Journey
of a
Prayer Warrior

by Jill Wischhusen

DEDICATION

This book is dedicated to the man I love the most – JESUS!

CONTENTS

About this book   i

1   Childhood   1

2   Salvation   5

3   Growth   11

4   Victories   25

5   Ministry Opportunities   31

6   A New Mission Field   35

7   Prayers and Next Steps   45

8   One Final Question   73

9   Journal   75

For More Information and to Share Your Story   106

ABOUT THIS BOOK

This book is about my journey, but it's also about yours.

It's written in the same way you would speak to a friend sitting across the kitchen table: simple, straightforward, and honest.

I encourage you to read this book through more than once, then use the journal in the back to record your own journey.

1
CHILDHOOD

I was born into a middle class family in a very small town. My parents were both alcoholics and were well known by everyone in town. My very first childhood memories are of my father coming into my bedroom while I was in the crib crying, and he spanked me - telling me to be quiet. (I spent a lot of time in that prison...I mean "crib.")

As I grew older, the beatings became much more intense. It seemed like my parents hated me. They never treated my brother or sister the same way they treated me. It was a normal day for my father to come home, have a drink, and then punch me in the face or throw me across the room. I can still remember balls of my hair lying on the floor. I thought I did such horrible things and deserved the beatings.

I was told I would never be worth anything and at one point they told me that someone was coming to take me away. They made me sit on a chair and wait. This was some strange fear factor. I don't know what I did, but they wanted me gone. I was around 7 when this happened, sitting on the chair waiting for the new people who were going to save me. They never came, of course. It was the longest hour on a chair in my life.

On other occasions my parents would lock me in the basement or pretend to play hide and seek in the attic as they locked the door behind them. I was petrified! There were bats up there! I looked out the little window and saw my mom leaving the house. How could she have forgotten me?

The drunken rampages became more and more frequent. I would hear my father come home and would run and hide under my bed. I actually spent a lot of time under there, gripped in a fear that literally paralyzed me.

One of the most difficult things is that I never knew if each day would be a good day or bad day. I remember being under the bed in my darkest moment, begging God to just kill me and get it over with. I heard nothing. Even God was mad at me, I thought.

I was too scared to run away, because if I got caught and had to go back they would kill me. No matter what I did, it was not good enough. I looked for any way I could to get out of that place I called hell.

I was raised in the Catholic Church. Not with my parents - they stayed home and drank. I spent as much time in church as I could. I asked the priest if I could clean the church for free just to stay away from home. My parents didn't seem to have any problems with me spending so much time there. I wanted to tell the priest how bad it was, but out of fear of it getting back to them, I just kept my mouth shut. I couldn't tell a soul, because my parents would kill me if they found out.

I would go to school with bruises and fat lips, and teachers would ask me if I was okay. I didn't dare tell them the truth. I loved school because it was a safe place. I did as much outside of the house as possible. Out of sight out of mind, I suppose.

As I got older and into my teenage years, the beatings became more violent. The worst night of my life was the night my parents had been out drinking. When they got home they were drunk, and my father came right after me. He grabbed me off the couch and threw me on the ground, climbed on top of me and started to choke me to death. I lay there in shock and helpless. I was convinced this was my last day on earth, and all I could do at this point was just pray for God to help me.

All of a sudden there was a strange look in my father's eyes and he stopped. I ran for my life and hid under the bed. *How could a father do this to his daughter? How could God allow him to do this to me?* These were the questions I constantly asked myself. Didn't he love me? *No one loved me*, I thought. The entire family knew about the abuse, but no one wanted to get involved.

Jill Wischhusen

2
SALVATION

I went to church every week, but it was more like a social get-together. I don't remember anything except two prayers: Hail Mary and Our Father. I didn't own a Bible. I was brought up being told by my mother that God was always watching me and would "get" me if I did something wrong. More fear in my life is not what I needed.

I grew up never satisfied with anything about myself and I sure didn't love myself. I had believed them when they told me I was worthless. I started smoking marijuana to try to ease the pain of being hated by them all. I thought it helped me to cope, but it was just covering up the problem.

Finally God answered my prayers and sent me a knight in shining armor! He was an officer in the military and just fell head over heels for me. I wasn't used to anyone being nice to me. He bought me nice things, flowers, told me he loved me and then he asked me to marry him. I said yes before he could even get the rest of the words out of his mouth! I was breaking free from hell! I thought that this might change my parents' attitude towards me and now (since I was grown up), they would be able to accept me and love me. That didn't happen. I never was beat up again, but they still did a lot of mental and verbal abuse in front of my new husband. He didn't even know how to deal with this because he came from a tight-knit family. Soon we had our first baby - still no acceptance from my parents. I had to just accept the fact that these people hated me.

Married life to a sailor was not as easy as I thought it would be. He was on submarines and his job took him out to sea on long 6-month long deployments.

I spent holidays and birthdays alone. It was that same alone feeling I had before, but this time I had to be responsible for another human. *How can I love this child when I don't know what love is?* I sought out help from social services, and I told them my past and that I was worried about this abuse coming out in me. I didn't ever want to hurt my children like I was hurt. They assured me it would not happen because I was aware of the problem.

I was going to a Catholic Church with the kids every week and I really don't know why, maybe it was because I still felt like if I didn't God would get me. I was really a non-practicing Catholic.

Things were spinning out of control every time my husband went out to sea. It was just so much responsibility to do this all by myself with no help or family support. Unfortunately, the marriage only lasted 9 years. It was so lonely. I tried counseling and nothing worked. We got legally separated. I met a man at the shoe store I was working in and he told me that he was also legally separated. He asked if I wanted to go on a date. "Sure, why not?" I replied.

We went out and had a great time. He started to see me more and more, until one day someone came to my door. I had a friend over at the time and when I opened the door there was this beautiful woman who looked just like an angel. She had long, flowing blonde hair and a petite body; she was shining.

She said, "Hello, Jill, I am Barbara. Steve's wife." All I could think was that she was there to kill me. My next immediate thought was that I couldn't believe he left her. I was shocked and didn't know what to do, so I invited her in.

She told me they were not separated and that he had lied! I was shocked and felt like I was violated. She was so sweet. How could this woman be so nice if she thought I was stealing her husband? My friend sat there and just listened to us. We talked for a while and then she looked me in the eyes and said, "Can I ask you a question?" I said sure, and she replied, "If you were to die today, do you know where you're going?"

"Of course I do," I said, "I am going to Heaven."

She asked me, "How can you be sure?" I said I would because I was Catholic and I had never hurt a thing in my life and I was a good person. She asked if she could show me something. I said that she could, and she opened her purse and pulled out a pocket size Bible. I thought to myself, *Oh, God. A*

Bible thumper.

But then she showed me the scripture in John 14:6: "Jesus answered, 'I am the way and the truth and the life. No one comes to the Father except through me.'" I really didn't know what she was trying to say, and I surely didn't understand this scripture. She said, "Do you want to be sure that you're going to go to Heaven?" I said I absolutely did, and she said, "Would you like to say the prayer of salvation and accept Jesus into your life so you can be with God in Heaven?"

I repeated the prayer and she congratulated me, and my friend starting to scream hallelujah! I was not understanding why this was such a big deal. They said Heaven was celebrating because I just accepted Jesus as my very own personal savior and they both hugged me and congratulated me and even called me their sister. She gave me a hug and left.

My mouth was still on the floor - what had just happened here? To this very day she has been so much influence and the best example to me of what a Christian should be like. I will always be grateful to her.

Later that night I lay in bed, I couldn't sleep. My mind was racing. All I could think about was that prayer. Was that all I had to do to go to Heaven? I didn't need to go to confession anymore? No more Lent? This seemed way to easy.

I lay in bed and said, "God I hope you heard my

prayer because I really want to know you." The door bell rang in an instant. My bed was right to the window, and I looked out and no one was there. I thought it was odd. How could anyone move away that quickly from the door?

At that time all of a sudden it felt like electricity going through my body. It started at the top of my head and went all the way to my feet. It lasted for what felt like an eternity. It didn't hurt; it actually reminded me of when I smoked too much marijuana and my head would get a rush. I thought to myself after it ended, "This is better than any drug I have ever smoked."

Then suddenly I was crying, the tears soaking my pillow. I really didn't know then why I was crying so hard, but it lasted for three days. I look back now and know that God was cleansing me from all of my sins and past.

The next day I got up and felt like I needed to throw away some things. I threw out all of the drugs and alcohol. I decided to get it out of the house. I told a few people what had happened the day before and none of them commented. One of them actually came over and took the stuff out of my trash can. Another friend came over that week and said the Lord's name in vain and it went through my veins like acid. It physically made me sick to my stomach. I was surprised that it had affected me like this because "Jesus, Mary, and Joseph" was my favorite saying.

Something was changing in me. This proved to me the word of God is true. "Therefore, if anyone is in Christ, he is a new creation; the old has gone, the new has come!" 2 Corinthians 5:17.

3
GROWTH

I wasn't really sure what my next course of action should be, but I knew I had to get a Bible. I never had a need for one before then, but now it was different. I remember that there was one in the house when I was growing up. I remember it was a huge book and it had everyone's obituary in it.

"Therefore, if anyone is in Christ, he is a new creation; the old has gone, the new has come!" I was a new creation, so I went on a quest to buy a Bible.

It was crazy, so many to choose from. I picked a pink Precious Moments Bible, because it was the prettiest one in the store. I brought it home and thought, *Now what? Where do I begin?* I opened to the book of John, with the thoughts I didn't need to know the old stuff, I should stick with the New Testament.

It was all Greek to me. I didn't understand a word. I grew frustrated and said "God you need to show me what to do with this. I don't get it, I need help." Then I randomly opened my Bible and looked down at what stuck out. The scripture that popped out was "Obey me and do everything I command you, and

you will be my people, and I will be your God."
Jeremiah 11:4.

I got scared and thought back to what my mother
had told me. God is "gonna get me" if I do anything
wrong. I had to see if this was just a fluke or what,
so I did it again. I closed the Bible and said, "God, if
that was just from you, prove it and do it again." The
next scripture I opened to was "So I say to you: Ask
and it will be given to you; seek and you will find;
knock and the door will be opened to you. for
everyone who asks receives; he who seeks finds;
and to him who knocks, the door will be opened."
Luke 11:9-10.

It was in red, so I thought it had to be important. I
just started crying because I felt like God was talking
to me. This could not be a coincidence. I liked this
communication thing with God! I even thought I was
one step ahead of myself because I already feared
The Lord, like the Bible said we should do.

Since I really had no knowledge of Jesus except he
was a really nice statue and he died on the cross, I
needed to investigate further. It turned into a
craving. I couldn't get enough. My friends all stopped
hanging around with me because I no longer smoked
or would drink with them. When I threw my stuff
out, they came and took it out of my trash. They
called me a "Jesus Freak"! All I could think of was
the day I thought Barbara was a Bible thumper. I felt
bad that I thought that about her.

I started to attend a Baptist church because of a recommendation from the friend that was at my house the day I turned my life over to The Lord. The first day I went, I was nervous and scared. I didn't know anyone, but they all seemed very nice and came over and introduced themselves and talked to me like they already knew me. I remember thinking, *Wow, these people are really nice.*

One woman came up to me and asked if I was new and if I wanted to join Sunday School. I told her I would let her know. (Sunday school? I thought that was for little kids! Why do I need that?) Then the music started and I really liked it. Much different from what I grew up with.

At the end of the service the pastor asked if anyone wanted Jesus in their life; if they did, they should come forward. I got right up and went down to the front. I felt kinda weird because the entire church was watching me. When I arrived at the altar, for some reason I was crying again. I said the prayer and they whisked me back behind the altar. They explained what I had just done. Then the woman told me that I needed to get water baptized. I told her I had been baptized as a baby.

She said that wasn't my choice and I had not personally made this declaration about The Lord. The next week I was scheduled for my baptism. I was set up in my Sunday School class that they said will help me understand things better. The next Sunday, I showed up in the Sunday school class. (I was pleasantly surprised that I was with adults and not children.) They all welcomed me like I was a celebrity. I told them I was going to be baptized that day. Everyone cheered and said they would be there to witness it. That took away some of the fear of what I was getting into.

After the service I was prepared for the baptism, and I was so nervous for some reason. I walked down and the pastor baptized me, dunking my entire body under water. I started to cry again when it was finished because the entire church of about 150 people cheered when I came up. I felt like a million bucks. I came home and called several members of my family to tell them the great news. They were unresponsive. (The first time they kept their mouths shut about anything in my life.) I was disappointed that they couldn't feel my joy and celebrate with me, but they didn't want anything to do with it. I could feel them talking about me, but I didn't care.

I went to every Sunday school class, Bible study, college classes, and crusade I could find. I went to church in the morning and evening - any time there were services, I was there. Sometimes I would go to 3 churches in one day. It didn't matter what church, I just wanted more. I was and still am addicted to The Lord. The more I studied, the deeper my relationship with Jesus grew. God still helped me along when I would ask Him a question and open my Bible and there before me was the answer. I loved that He answers me!! He really does exist.

One Sunday, I was in Sunday school and the leader of the class asked me if I would pray. I almost got sick. I really thought I was going to throw up right in front of everyone. My hands we're sweating, I kept feeling like I could not do it. I only knew the Hail Mary, Our Father and the rosary. I was on the verge of panic and I prayed, God speak thru me, I don't know how to do this. I prayed a general thank you for everyone and our salvation prayer. Then I felt really bad the rest of the day. I was embarrassed that I didn't really know how to pray. *What are they all thinking about me?* I wondered.

Reluctantly I went back to Sunday school the next week, and the leader took me aside before we started. I was scared he was kicking me out of the class because I didn't know how to pray, and if I couldn't do that, then I shouldn't be there.

He said, "Jill, I just want to tell you the prayer you said last week really touched my heart. Thank you for praying." I had to hold back the tears. He said everything opposite of what I had felt. That was the day I learned that Satan was trying to put fear and lies in me. As a new Christian it is so hard because of not knowing everything the "experienced" Christians know.

Once I was asked what was my favorite book in the Bible. I was still trying to figure out what to read. I told them all of it, thinking that would be safe. The more I studied the word of God the more revelation I had. I checked out the church that was closer to my house one Sunday. The pastor stopped the service and said, "I have a word for someone," and proceeded to point at me. I looked around to see who it could be and he said, "No, you." I pointed at myself and he nodded. (Wow, I didn't know what was going to happen.)

He said, "My daughter, I have prepared you for this time. I have put a sword in your right hand a long time ago and you, my daughter, will go to the nations and teach warfare prayer." It was strange because it registered with my spirit. It's like I already knew that but didn't. The funny thing is I had a sword that I used to twirl when I was a band front captain. But the warfare prayer part was something I had never heard of before.

He taped the entire word and gave it to me at the end of the service. I was excited that God spoke to me!!! I was so glad he taped it, because I was crying when he was talking and knew I wouldn't remember the whole word. I just put it in the back of my head and thought, *If it's your will, God.*

Soon after, a friend invited me to a Bible study in church called Breaking Free (with Beth Moore). It was an true awakening in my life. That was when I learned of generational curses in my life. These things needed to be dealt with.

Galatians 3:13 "But Christ has rescued us from the curse pronounced by the law. When he was hung on the cross, he took upon himself the curse for our wrongdoing. For it is written in the Scriptures, 'Cursed is everyone who is hung on a tree.'" I commanded every curse from the generations before me to flee and declared they are all broken and will no longer go through the generations of my family.

This study showed me not only were there generational curses but also a deeper understanding what Jesus died for on the cross. Boy, did I have some generational curses! I knew there was alcoholism/addiction in my family and saw how it came down through me with the drugs and alcohol.

Further, I was enlightened to my family's involvement in the occult. My mother played with a Ouija board and my grandfather was a Mason. I had no idea that this went down the generations to me as I had had psychic parties. From there it tried to attach to my daughter who started listening to Marilyn Manson and getting into occult-type mutilation. I was stunned to see how these curses and strongholds had gone through the generations. One of my relatives was very prejudiced towards African-Americans. She really hated them. That had tried to come onto me. I started to hate them because of her.

I repented for the things I did and was reminded that I broke all the curses when I claimed that Jesus is Lord in my life and from this point forward all generations after me will be free from the curses, strongholds and bondage. I wanted to be sure that my kids would be free.

I went to my children's rooms and I anointed everything! Their hairbrushes, pillows, shoes, keys, clothes. I knelt by their beds when they were not home and prayed away all further demonic curses. The anointing oil was used with prayers of protection, safety and peace. Then I thought *well, I can't let this stuff come through the front door.* I anointed the doors to the house and declared the blood of Jesus that was shed for me is now on the house, the doors, and anyone or thing that tries to come in won't be able to cross the blood line. I was taking authority over my house.

After I was done, I walked around and I heard a voice in my spirit to clean out the house of any idols. I remembered the verse in the Bible "Do not bring a detestable thing into your house or you, like it, will be set apart for destruction. Regard it as vile and utterly detest it, for it is set apart for destruction." Deuteronomy 7:26.

I thought I misunderstood because I didn't think I had anything unclean or idols. I walked around and said, "God show me what is not from you and needs to go." First thing He made me see was the sculpture on my fireplace mantle that was given to me from a friend who was an art major. It was made in Africa. Something was just not right with this sculpture. I only had it on the mantle so she would see that I was appreciative of her gift. But every time I looked at it I got a weird feeling. It had to go.

Then I went into the kitchen. I opened up the desk

drawer and I had forgotten that I had thrown one of those Jehovah Witness magazines in the drawer. It had to go! I was then directed to go under the kitchen sink, right in the front was a bottle of "holy water" the psychic had given me from one of her parties.

I was reminded of this scripture: "Let no one be found among you who sacrifices their son or daughter in the fire, who practices divination or sorcery, interprets omens, engages in witchcraft, or casts spells, or who is a medium or spiritist or who consults the dead. Anyone who does these things is detestable to the Lord; because of these same detestable practices the Lord your God will drive out those nations before you. You must be blameless before the Lord your God." Deuteronomy 18:10-13.

She had given me crosses, but I remember she told me she had an Indian chief as her medium. I even found religious medals and the rosary that I used to pray to. I was shocked to see that I had ended up with an entire trash bag filled with stuff that was detestable before God. I couldn't get it out of my house quick enough. I just kept asking God to forgive me.

I finished the inside, but what about the outside? I didn't want anything not from God on my land. I don't know what exactly was here 100 years ago and I thought back to the scripture "I will give you every place where you set your foot, as I promised Moses." Joshua 1:3

I went outside and walked all four corners of my land and declared that it was mine and I was covering it with the Blood of Jesus. Nothing can come on this land without Gods permission. Anything that was bad on the land that is under my feed needed to flee in Jesus name.

During the Breaking Free study, I found that I was doing something really wrong. I used to ask God to forgive me for my past sins. It was brought to my attention that I didn't trust God! I used to keep repenting on sins God had wiped out. I missed the part of He wiped it out, cleaned the slate, forgot! I kept reminding Him until He showed me this, "Repent, then, and turn to God, so that your sins may be wiped out, that times of refreshing may come from the Lord," Acts 3:19. I finally got it! It's really finished once you ask Him to forgive you.

So, I cleaned the inside of the house and the outside of the house, but I had one last problem. My husband, Paul, was unsaved. I took him to church with me one time and he had to leave to go throw up. I knew this was going to be hard. He had seen me changing the entire time we have been married and made snide little comments under his breath calling me names, saying I was not a Christian and telling me I was a liar. I put up with this for years.

He had the same familiar spirit as my dad, but I did not realize it until we were married. He slapped me around a lot when he was drinking. He was verbally abusive and treated me like very badly. Once again,

I found myself living in fear like I had with my father. I just kept my mouth shut to keep the peace.

One day he had a bad migraine and I told him of he would surrender it to God and ask The Lord into his life He would take it away. He told me he didn't want to because he wanted to go to hell with all of his friends. As he was saying this I noticed his sky blue eyes went black.

I was taken back by his comment but managed to get out of my mouth "Well, while you and all your buddies are down in hell eating Oreos, I will be upstairs with the milk. You will be parched and want my milk then!"

He said a few choice cuss words and I rebuked him and walked away. I went home and prayed and said to myself, *this is MY house!* When I said "house," the scripture, "But if serving the LORD seems undesirable to you, then choose for yourselves this day whom you will serve, whether the gods your ancestors served beyond the Euphrates, or the gods of the Amorites, in whose land you are living. But as for me and my household, we will serve the LORD." Joshua 24:15.

I shouted out to Satan, "This is my household and WE WILL ALL SERVE THE LORD!" I had decided I had enough of this demon running wild in my house using my own husband against me! "For our struggle is not against flesh and blood, but against the rulers, against the authorities, against the powers of this dark world and against the spiritual forces of evil in the heavenly realms." Ephesians 6:12

I needed to take authority over this demon. The word of God says, "I have given you authority to trample on snakes and scorpions and to overcome all the power of the enemy; nothing will harm you." Luke 10:19.

Paul came home from work and soon after he came in the door he told me I was a hypocrite, that I am not saved - and from that point I stopped listening. He headed out to the garage and I followed him. I walked up to him and slammed his body against the wall! I looked into his black eyes and said, "I know who you are and you are not getting my husband." I slammed him against the wall again and said, "Get out of my husband right now in the name of Jesus!" (Paul actually looked scared!) I screamed at the top of my lungs "Believe in The Lord Jesus, and you will be saved-you and your household!! (Acts 16:31) I screamed, "This is MY household, my ground and my husband in the name of Jesus Christ of Nazareth, I command you to flee!"

As soon as I said that and covered him for the top of his head to the soles of his feet with the Blood of Jesus, his eyes turned blue again! That weekend Paul and I went to church, Paul walked down the aisle, and turned his life over to The Lord. One of the best days in my life.

Within days I saw a complete change in Paul. I have

to admit I surprised myself that day. I had put up with so much, I broke out of the fear! The root to fear is death. I don't fear death anymore. I actually look forward to the day I see Jesus.

Jill Wischhusen

4
VICTORIES

I still had one more obstacle, my abusive father.
How can I honor someone who beat me so badly and
hated me so deeply? I asked around and no one
could really answer my question about if it was okay
that I don't honor him. I felt horrible because it's one
of the Ten Commandments. I felt like I was living in
sin.

I prayed and prayed. What do I do? It was another
one of those moments when God had me open up
the Bible and look down. There was my answer!!!
This made the hairs on my neck stand up! "Therefore
I tell you, whatever you ask for in prayer, believe
that you have received it, and it will be yours. And
when you stand praying, if you hold anything against
anyone, forgive them, so that your Father in heaven
may forgive you your sins." Mark 11:24-25.

It was as if He put this there just for me!! Now, how
do I forgive him? It sounded easy, but it was the
hardest thing I have had to figure out in my life. But,
I got it! It was not my dad beating me! My battle
was not against his flesh and blood! It was the
enemy using him to get rid of me because he knew
God had plans for me. That is why he tried to crush
my spirit and make be feel like a prisoner from birth!

It was never my dad! It was the most freeing moment in my life and I am able to forgive everyone now! It's not the flesh coming against us!

I contacted my dad and told him I wanted to visit him. When I got there, immediately I was questioned about my "religion". First I was asked if I play with snakes in my church? I told him no, that I only step on their heads when given the opportunity. Then the next question was, "How could you turn your back from the Catholic Church?" I tried to explain that it's not about any church or religion, it is about the relationship you have with God. He didn't get it. The night before I left, I was lead to write him a letter telling him how to be sure he would go to Heaven.

The next morning we got in the car and headed to the airport. We didn't speak one word. Halfway there he blurts out, "You're not a Christian! You're a hypocrite!"

I immediately recognized the enemy's voice. I heard this line before! He put his hand towards my face. I screamed, "Satan, I rebuke you! Get off my father"! He screamed some more, and I screamed back, "I am not scared of you anymore! I have been set free from Fear!"

"There is no fear in love; but perfect love casts out fear: because fear has torment. He that fears is not made perfect in love." John 4:18. This was the very first time I was in a place alone with my father when I was not shaking and panic- stricken. I told him that

I was a Christian and that is how I was able to forgive him for all the years of abuse. I told him I loved him. We arrived at the airport and he threw my luggage on the curb, got in his car and said, "Have a nice life."

I watched him drive off. I wasn't sad - I actually felt like the entire earth had been lifted off my chest! That was the last time I saw my father. He will not talk to me still and it has been over 10 years. I left the letter on his car seat as I was getting out of the car and I am claiming my father's salvation. He was part of the household I was in and God put him in my life on purpose.

The rest of my family won't talk to me either. They all call me a Jesus Freak! I love it - that means they noticed my love for The Lord. I pray for them every day and have no unforgiveness, but it does feel really good that I am not under that attack anymore.

When I returned Paul and I were given the names of a spiritual couple that works with couples one on one doing in depth Bible studies. Bob and Audrey, whom we call our spiritual parents, were sent to us from God. We went to their house weekly and they discussed situations we were going through and went through the Bible with us and taught us the scriptures and meaning in depth.

Bob was telling us one night that he was sitting on God's lap and God was speaking to him. I couldn't believe this was the same God. I thought He was really mean. My biological father was and I was always told he was gonna get me if I was bad. How could this be that you could sit on His lap?

Bob is who really changed my thoughts on who God really is. He is not mean. He has his arms open wide and wants me to sit on His lap, too. I cried so hard, thinking *He really does love me*. The word proves it and Bob just confirmed it. That was the day I really received the love that I had been hidden from. He revealed Himself! If Bob had not told me about his encounter with my Heavenly Father, I would not have grasped who He really is. I had been brought up with the wrong fear of God. My fear now is when I do something that is not right, I don't want to hurt Him in anyway. I just want to bless Him with everything I do. He made me so He knows I am not prefect but, He doesn't care, He loves me unconditionally.

One of the biggest issues we fell victim to is what we were saying. We were cursing ourselves with our own tongues. "The tongue has the power of life and death, and those who love it will eat it's fruit." Proverbs 18:21. Simple things, like saying your sick and tired, gave Satan power. We could not believe how much bad stuff we were calling in.

We will never say we are broke again. There is a dime in the couch somewhere! We were speaking against God's word which says, "For I know the plans I have for you," declares the LORD, "plans to prosper you and not to harm you, plans to give you hope and a future." Jeremiah 29:11.

Now we check each other and only speak truth. God has equipped us for His purpose. I started to pray that God would reveal His purpose in my life. The one thing I did know is I have so much compassion for hurting people. Sometimes I would stop by the store on the way home from church, get flowers, and just walk into any random nursing home. I was never questioned, just signed in. I would go to the rooms and hand each one a flower and tell them Jesus sent me to tell them He loves them. He didn't really actually tell me to go, I just felt led. He loves everyone! No matter how young or old, good or bad.

According to Acts: 10:34: "Then Peter began to speak: 'I now realize how true it is that God does not show favoritism.'" I also know His word says, "The Lord is not slow in keeping his promise, as some understand slowness. Instead he is patient with you, not wanting anyone to perish, but everyone to come to repentance." 2Peter 3:9. The word also says, "The thief comes only to steal and kill and destroy; I have come that they may have life, and have it to the full." John 10:10.

A lot of people thought God was mad at them and sent them there to die. It made me weep, but I am glad I could show them that wasn't true. God loved them.

Jill Wischhusen

5
MINISTRY OPPORTUNITIES

A friend was working at a local soup kitchen and I asked if she would mind if I went. I loved it! The place was filled with hopeless people who came hungry. I was there to feed them spiritually.

One day a man walked in the door with a marijuana cigarette sticking out of his beard! I asked him what he was going to do with it? He told me he was going to smoke it after dinner. I asked him if it was any good. I loved it that I knew all about this subject! He said it was okay. I asked him if he wanted to know where to get the really good stuff? I told him he would get so high and never get the munchies. His eyes lit right up and he asked where he could find it.

I pointed up. I told him about the night I gave my life to The Lord and how high I felt and I haven't come down since. He looked interested. I asked him if he wanted in? He said, "Yes, I do." I prayed the prayer of salvation with him, he asked God for forgiveness, and then he wept.

On the way out he hugged me and thanked me and then threw the joint in the trash. I went back the next week and he came to tell me he wasn't eating there today. He said he went to church that weekend and God gave him a job. I asked him if he was still smoking weed and he told me the night he threw it in the trash was the last time he smoked. Hallelujah! I said, "So if the Son sets you free, you will be free indeed." John 8:36. He was set free that night.

A couple months later, I was asked if I wanted to pray for the girls in the Juvenile detention center. I prayed and went. My purpose!!! The girls have been abused, on drugs, some did bad things to get away from being raped by family members, and they felt safe there. All were told they would not have a good future because of their past actions.

Who would have ever thought that all the abuse I went through would be used to talk to these young women to tell them I knew exactly where they were at? I told them the feelings I had and several cried. They needed to hear that God has plans for them and this was not His destiny for them but a part of their life that He would use to help others later.

I prayed over them that they would be able to come back and help the others coming in. God used my past to set the girls free! Twelve of them gave their lives to The Lord. One told me she was in witchcraft. My testimony of being set free from the curses of the occult set her free that night.

They asked me for Bibles, and I highlighted all twelve with scriptures that got me to where I am today. It was one of the satisfying moments in my life. God was revealing my purpose. A few months later, I kept hearing the word mission in my head. The funny thing about that is I won't even drive to the next city. He couldn't possibly be talking to me, could He? Was this the prophetic word coming to fruition?

Jill Wischhusen

6
A NEW MISSION FIELD

At the same time I was hearing that word, I was watching a show called *Life Today* on the Christian network. They showed these poor little kids in Africa starving to death. All they need is water and they would be able to grow food and have a clean drinking supply. I wept watching these poor children. It just broke my heart. I said, God if you give me the $2500, for the well, I will send it. It was the beginning of January. Every time I turned this show on, I was reminded how good we have it and continued to weep for the children. All I could think of daily was about those poor children - I just couldn't get them off my mind.

In the meantime, one of my friends called me. She said that God told her to give me a word. (Of course I test every word to make sure it lines up with the word of God.) She said, "God wants you to go on the mission field." (I guess He had to tell her to tell me because I tend to be a little thick-headed.)

I said to her that it was funny she said that because I kept having the word "mission" pop up in my head. I thanked her for the word and hung up the phone.

The next day another friend called me and said, "Did you know there is a missionary training camp in this area?" She said, "God is telling me you are to go."

Was she kidding me? Was He kidding me? I told her I really didn't think that was for me. But out of curiosity, I checked it out. The camp was hosted by the Elijah Company. I called just to see what they had going on. They told me the price and I didn't have the funds at the time to go.

After researching them, I told another close friend of mine about what had been going on, and she told me she wanted to give me the money to go. I couldn't believe she said that, but deep in my heart I knew God wanted me there.

I signed up and was almost scared of what we would be doing. I was pretty sure I was going to run through the forest with 50 lbs. of rice on my back. I didn't even really know what missionaries did, but I was about to take the class. The class was paid for, so I had to go now.

I arrived in the morning, but I was extremely exhausted from not sleeping at all the night before. My hands were sweating and I was nervous. There were only about 15 other people. We went way into the night, studying, worshiping and praising the Lord. I was so tired and really thought I could die right there in front of all of them from exhaustion.

Once we were finished, we all went back to our cabins. I was so relieved we didn't run through the forest and thought to myself, *this isn't so bad*. That night as soon as I laid my head down on the pillow, a rooster sat outside of my window and crowed the entire night! I was past the point of exhaustion and then came the tears. The bird wouldn't shut up! It didn't seem to bother anyone but me. (Maybe because it was right outside *my* window.)

I moaned, groaned and at one point I wanted to hunt it down and kill it! I could feel the anger welling up inside of me. I did not sleep at all that night.

The next morning I packed my stuff up and was going to leave. I needed sleep and that was all there was to it. I didn't want to do this anymore. I went into the building and told the leaders that I was leaving and thanked them for having me.

They wanted to know why I wanted to leave and I told them what had happened and that I just couldn't do this. The entire group put me in the center and started to pray for me. All of a sudden, I felt wide awake. I said, "I'll stay!" (Now I know it was because Satan didn't want me to hear what they had to say.)

I stayed the three days. The last day of the camp a beautiful woman of God, who is a prophetess, came to give each of us a word from The Lord. I couldn't wait until it was my turn. What was He gonna say? She called me up and said almost the same exact word that I had heard that day in church. Once again, I had the sword in my right hand and I would go to the nations to teach warfare prayer and many would be saved and healed.

This was a confirmation to me that I was really going to do some sort of mission. The next Sunday, I went to the church and the funniest thing happened. A woman came up to me and said our church is going on a mission trip to Ukraine and wanted to know if I could come. I must have looked like I had just seen a ghost. I could feel my blood drain to my feet. She asked me if I was okay. I said, "Let me pray on it and I will get back to you."

This was so bizarre! This couldn't be a coincidence. God had been preparing me.

Ephesians 2:10 "For we are God's handiwork, created in Christ Jesus to do good works, which God prepared in advance for us to do."

I prayed and told God, "I am fully surrendered, teach me, lead me and use me wherever you need me." Then I prayed and said, "God, tell me what You want, not what I would want." I opened my Bible right to the scripture, "Then I heard the voice of the Lord saying, 'Whom shall I send? And who will go for us?' And I said, 'Here am I. Send me!'" Isaiah 6:8.

I cried like a baby. I told God, "I will go. Send me. But, can you give me a confirmation? I want to make sure I am hearing you and not the voice of another."

A few weeks went by and it was Good Friday. I received a check for $2500!!! The African kids are getting a well!!! I ran to the TV to get the number to call in and make the donation. I wanted to hurry before something happened and I would have it disappear. I turned the channel to *Life Today*. There was a problem. Where were the African kids? They had been on the TV almost every day. But today they were not.

I listened and they were talking about an orphanage. I thought those poor little kids abandoned. I knew how that felt. Then they said the orphanage was in Ukraine!!! Did I just hear them right!? I stopped right in my tracks! Was this the confirmation I was looking for? A small voice inside of me said, "sow into that place before you get there". But what about the African kids? My heart was set on helping them. I said, "God if you want me to give this $2500 to them, then I need another confirmation."

They announced the name of the orphanage, the Joshua house, and my son Joshua walked in the door at the exact moment they said the name. I cried so hard I could barely speak. I felt like God just put His hand right on my head! My son asked what was wrong, and I couldn't tell him because I was crying too hard. I finally was able to make the call. I still don't know how they could understand me through all the sobs, but they did. I asked if I could get the information regarding this orphanage because I was going there. They freely gave me the information.

I went to church on Sunday and told the leader of the mission trip, that I was going to go, that I heard from God, and He wants me there. He gave me information regarding the meeting for what is needed. Then I wrote an email to the Joshua house and said I was coming and I would like to visit them if it would be okay. They wrote back and said they needed to pray on it for the children's safety.

I went to lunch that week with a friend, and I didn't tell anyone what God had told me, except for the mission leader and the orphanage. She sat down and handed me an envelope. She said, "God told me to give this to you and you would know what it was for."

I opened the envelope and it had a $500 check in it!! I broke down at the table. I told her everything! She quoted the scripture, "And how can anyone preach unless they are sent? As it is written: 'How beautiful are the feet of those who bring good news!'" Romans 10:15.

I got home and I was shaking, my hands were sweating, and I couldn't believe I was really going to do this. Reality had hit me when I got the check. I sat down and was thinking about the whole thing and got scared. I said, "God, you know I won't even drive to the next town...are you sure you want me in the Ukraine?" It was like He was sending me to another planet. I said, "God, do you really need me in the Ukraine? Can't you use me in Jamaica?"

I didn't hear a word. Before you know it, I had been given money from so many people, I had more than enough for the trip. People who didn't even have a relationship with The Lord just handed me money. It was so surprising. Not everyone thought it was a good idea that I would go to Ukraine. My relatives were all opposed. Told me I was nuts and God would not send me there. (Several told me I was nuts to go.) This was all driven by their own fears.

A few days before the trip, I received word back from the Joshua House - they said I was free to come visit. I called my mission leader and told him I had sown a seed into an orphanage in Ukraine and was wondering if we could stop by while we are there. He asked where it was and I told him the location. He said that we would be nowhere near that place, that it was all the way in the other side of the country. I said, "Well, God told me to sow into the place before I got there, but maybe I misunderstood."

The day or so before we were set to leave the leader called me. He said, "Jill, do you still want to go to the orphanage?" I said, "Yes, why?" He said that city had just called and asked if they could send a team!!!

The phone fell out of my hands and I went down on my knees! God was up to something BIG!! I cried, laughed, cried, and laughed more! What was He going to do? All I know is Satan was scared to death!

The warfare that I endured before I left was every one of my biggest fears. The day before I left I received a letter from the IRS, saying I owed $44,000 for years past and I had 10 days to address it!

All I could say is G. O. D. is bigger than I.R.S.

I called and said I was leaving and needed an extension 'til I got back. Then my head started to itch, I looked in the mirror and I had HEADLICE! No one in the family had it except for me. My kids had it when they were small and when I was not in a relationship with The Lord. It was the worst thing that I thought I could experience. It had a stigma that you were unclean if you got them.

I had a an allergic reaction to one of the shots given to me for the trip two days before. And to top it all off, my kids were spinning out of control. Thank goodness I recognized where it was all coming from and did not cancel my trip, which is exactly what Satan wanted. He was trying to send the spirit of fear at me.

Until the day I got on the plane, I asked for confirmations regarding going on this trip. At any time God could change his mind. It was really amusing how He gave me these confirmations. A prospective client called and where do you think he was from? Ukraine. Someone showed up at my door to sell me something, where were they from? Ukraine! I turned on the news, Ukraine. I am pretty sure God laughs at me. But, He also made me, so He knows how thick-headed I can be. Regardless, He was sending me to Ukraine! I had no idea what He wanted me there for, but I couldn't wait to find out!

...36 Seeing the people, He felt compassion for them, because they were distressed and dispirited like sheep without a shepherd. 37 Then He said to His disciples, "The harvest is plentiful, but the workers are few. 38 "Therefore beseech the Lord of the harvest to send out workers into His harvest." Matthew 9:36-38

Jill Wischhusen

7
PRAYERS AND NEXT STEPS

Salvation Prayer

I am going to ask you the same question I was asked, "If you were to die today, do you know without a doubt you will be going to Heaven?"

If your answer has even the slightest doubt and you never made a verbal statement asking Him into your life, please pray this simple prayer out loud. You have nothing to lose and an eternity of joy, peace and love to gain. It's a life changing event and when you say this prayer, all of Heaven stops and rejoices over your name being added to he Lambs Book of Life! That's right, there is an all out celebration!!!! It's your Birthday in Heaven!! If yes, have you already asked Jesus into your life? If so, maybe you don't have a relationship with Him that you can feel His breath on your face or hear Him whisper to you that He loves you. Just surrender and prayer this prayer again. He knows your heart and wants you to know His.

If you do not know Jesus as your Savior and Lord, simply pray the following prayer in faith, and Jesus will be your Lord!

"Heavenly Father, I come to you and ask Jesus to come into my heart and just take over my life. I completely surrender everything over to You Lord and ask that you take this mess and turn it into a message. I know that you died for me on the cross and you took all my sins and sickness. God raised You, Jesus , from the dead so that I could be saved. Please forgive me for my of the sins (I just let them all out!, if you miss some, it's okay, He already knows ;). And Lord, let them be remembered no more. From my heart and my mouth I confess this on (this day) _____, 20__, that Jesus Christ is Lord of my life! Thank You JESUS! AMEN!"

Sign here_____ , your name has just been written in the Lambs Book of Life at the same time Heaven!

NOW PUT A HUGE SMILE ON YOUR FACE!!! THIS IS THE BIGGEST DAY OF YOUR LIFE!!! CELEBRATE!!!!! Keep the date remembered! You just became a ROYAL! Your Father is the King of Kings! You have just been accepted as His son or daughter. You are a new creation!

Scripture references:

Speaking it out

John 14:6
6 Jesus answered, "I am the way and the truth and the life. No one comes to the Father except through me."

Acts 2:21
21 And everyone who calls on the name of the Lord will be saved.

Romans 10:9
9 If you declare with your mouth, "Jesus is Lord," and believe in your heart that God raised him from the dead, you will be saved.

Lamb's Book of Life

Philippians 4:3
3 Yes, and I ask you, my true companion, help these women since they have contended at my side in the cause of the gospel, along with Clement and the rest of my co-workers, whose names are in the book of life.

Revelation 3:5
5 The one who is victorious will, like them, be dressed in white. I will never blot out the name of that person from the book of life, but will

acknowledge that name before my Father and his angels.

Revelation 20:15
15 Anyone whose name was not found written in the book of life was thrown into the lake of fire.

Revelation 17:8
8 The beast, which you saw, once was, now is not, and yet will come up out of the Abyss and go to its destruction. The inhabitants of the earth whose names have not been written in the book of life from the creation of the world will be astonished when they see the beast, because it once was, now is not, and yet will come.

Revelation 13:8
8 All inhabitants of the earth will worship the beast— all whose names have not been written in the Lamb's book of life, the Lamb who was slain from the creation of the world.

Revelation 21:27
27 Nothing impure will ever enter it, nor will anyone who does what is shameful or deceitful, but only those whose names are written in the Lamb's book of life.

Celebration in Heaven

Luke 15:7
7 I tell you that in the same way there will be more

rejoicing in heaven over one sinner who repents than over ninety-nine righteous persons who do not need to repent.

Luke 15:10
10 In the same way, I tell you, there is rejoicing in the presence of the angels of God over one sinner who repents."

Royalty

Exodus 19:6
6 you[a] will be for me a kingdom of priests and a holy nation.' These are the words you are to speak to the Israelites."

Proverbs 25:2
2 It is the glory of God to conceal a matter; to search out a matter is the glory of kings.

Isaiah 62:3
3 You will be a crown of splendor in the Lord's hand, a royal diadem in the hand of your God.

1Peter 2:9
9 But you are a chosen people, a royal priesthood, a holy nation, God's special possession, that you may declare the praises of him who called you out of darkness into his wonderful light.

New creation

2 Corinthians 5:17
17 Therefore, if anyone is in Christ, the new creation has come:The old has gone, the new is here!

What exactly is Repentance

and why you need to do it

The definition from Webster's online Dictionary:

re·pent verb \ri-'pent\

- to feel or show that you are sorry for something bad or wrong that you did and that you want to do what is right.

In order to be forgiven we have to be genuinely sorry. This is where your heart completely changes. Once you have asked forgiveness for your sins and really mean it, a weight is lifted off your shoulders. This doesn't have to be shared with the world, it is just between you and The Lord. The Lord is the only ONE that took it on the cross for you.

This is what happens once you repent: not only do you feel completely free, but if you mess up (and you will) it will bother you. It won't be a guilt feeling - it will be a sad feeling that you did something that would not please The Lord. It hurts your heart. It happened to me as soon as I said the Lord's name in vain. I was beside myself that I did that.

This is what I describe as fear of The Lord. I am in fear of hurting him in any way. When I said His name in vain it was like acid going thru me. I cried because it bothered me so much. Very strange, since before I stepped into a relationship, His name was one of my favorites to use when I was mad. So what did I do after I did this? I asked Him to forgive me and help me not to allow the enemy to use my mouth against Him and if He needed to muzzle it, then He should!

Understand this: no one in this world is perfect and as a new believer in Jesus Christ, don't beat yourself up if you mess up. YOU'RE STILL NOT PERFECT. The difference is now you recognize that you messed up and repented.

Have you repented yet? Write down how you feel after you do it:

_____

_____

_____

_____

_____

_____

_____

_____

Beware of these Tricks from the pit:

Someone from your past will come along and remind you of something bad you did what, which will try to make you feel guilty.

You will feel like what you have done can't possibly be forgotten by God.

You will slip up! Maybe an accidental cuss word, maybe a white lie.

Your family will remind you about your sins!

Remind you over and over of the sins any way he can.

Repenting for the same thing you did over and over.

Scripture references:

REPENTANCE

Acts 3:19
19 Repent, then, and turn to God, so that your sins may be wiped out, that times of refreshing may come from the Lord,

Acts 17:30
30 In the past God overlooked such ignorance, but now he commands all people everywhere to repent.

Matthew 3:8
8 Produce fruit in keeping with repentance.

1 John 1:9
9 If we confess our sins, he is faithful and just and will forgive us our sins and purify us from all unrighteousness.

1 John 1:9
9 If we confess our sins, he is faithful and just and will forgive us our sins and purify us from all unrighteousness.

Mark 1:5
5 The whole Judean countryside and all the people of Jerusalem went out to him. Confessing their sins, they were baptized by him in the Jordan River.

Acts 2:38

38 Peter replied, "Repent and be baptized, every one of you, in the name of Jesus Christ for the forgiveness of your sins. And you will receive the gift of the Holy Spirit.

FORGIVEN

John 8:36

36 So if the Son sets you free, you will be free indeed.

2 Corinthians 3:17

Now the Lord is the Spirit, and where the Spirit of the Lord is, there is freedom.

Luke 7:48

48 Then Jesus said to her, "Your sins are forgiven."

How to equip yourself

First, you need a Bible. Most people don't have one or of they do it was given to them. I suggest you look in your area for a Christian Bookstore. If you don't have one, you can easily go online. Some churches will even supply a free Bible.

This Bible is going to be your book for life. You are going to use it like you use your shoes. You'll drop it, spill stuff on it and write in it. Get a Bible that you think will last for a long time. I originally had been given a King James Bible, but I just couldn't get past all the thou, arts, etc. For some reason it just was not easy reading for me. I brought the New International Version (NIV). It's very easy to understand. God knows how thick-headed some of us can be.

I was so embarrassed the first time I went to church, when the Pastor told me to look in the book of John and I had no idea where John was! The person next to me was kind enough to find it for me.

How can you avoid this? Get the Bible tabs. They are cheap and will make your life a lot easier! Another great items to get are a small notebook and highlighters that can highlight Bible pages.

Checklist:

Bible
Bible tabs
Small notebook
Bible highlighter pen

What Church to go to?

It's hard to figure out which church to go to in the beginning. All you know is what you may have grown up with or which churches you have heard stories about.

Some churches believe in salvation, some don't. Some believe in the saints, some believe in rituals. There are so many out there, it is hard to know. I recommend that you check out a few to see which one you feels most like family at. Just remember that everyone in the church is also not perfect. If someone cuts you off in the parking lot, don't freak out! They may have not have noticed you. Satan loves to see Christians fight, so always be on guard with your emotions.

Here are some things you should look for in a church:

1. What is their mission statement?

Do they believe that Jesus Christ is Lord, the son of God, and that He died on the cross for our sins and "sickness" and that on the 3rd day He rose from the dead? Do they believe in salvation? If not, you need to go right back out where you came in.

2. When the singing begins, is everyone sitting

down or just standing there mouthing the words? Is the joy of The Lord obvious in that place?

Acts 2:47
47 praising God and enjoying the favor of all the people. And the Lord added to their number daily those who were being saved.

3. Did they ask if anyone wanted to accept The Lord or be water baptized? What really is their purpose?

4. Do they have Sunday school classes for your age? If not, you will not learn a lot there.

Proverbs 1:5
5 let the wise listen and add to their learning,
and let the discerning get guidance—
2 Timothy3:14
14 But as for you, continue in what you have learned and have become convinced of, because you know those from whom you learned it,

5. Did they offer to pray for anyone? (If you needed prayer, wouldn't you want the church to pray for you?)

James 5:14
14 Is anyone among you sick? Let them call the elders of the church to pray over them and anoint them with oil in the name of the Lord.

6. Do they have church activities, woman's Bible studies, men's breakfast meetings?

This is great fellowship.

Acts 2:42
42 They devoted themselves to the apostles' teaching and to fellowship, to the breaking of bread and to prayer. 43 Everyone was filled with awe at the many wonders and signs performed by the apostles. 44 All the believers were together and had everything in common.

7. Do they believe in all the gifts?

1 Corinthians 12:1-11
12 Now about the gifts of the Spirit, brothers and sisters, I do not want you to be uninformed. 2 You know that when you were pagans, somehow or other you were influenced and led astray to mute idols. 3 Therefore I want you to know that no one who is speaking by the Spirit of God says, "Jesus be cursed," and no one can say, "Jesus is Lord," except by the Holy Spirit.
4 There are different kinds of gifts, but the same Spirit distributes them. 5 There are different kinds of service, but the same Lord. 6 There are different kinds of working, but in all of them and in everyone it is the same God at work.
7 Now to each one the manifestation of the Spirit is

given for the common good. 8 To one there is given through the Spirit a message of wisdom, to another a message of knowledge by means of the same Spirit, 9 to another faith by the same Spirit, to another gifts of healing by that one Spirit, 10 to another miraculous powers, to another prophecy, to another distinguishing between spirits, to another speaking in different kinds of tongues,[a] and to still another the interpretation of tongues.[b] 11 All these are the work of one and the same Spirit, and he distributes them to each one, just as he determines.

8. Finally, what does the church do for the community?

This will tell you where your if the church is producing good fruit.

Galatians 5:22-23
22 But the fruit of the Spirit is love, joy, peace, forbearance, kindness, goodness, faithfulness, 23 gentleness and self-control. Against such things there is no law.

All of these things are very important for your walk with Jesus. If they don't pray, will you be prayed for if you get sick?

If they are not doing anything for anyone, you will never grow into the calling God has for you.

If the preacher doesn't talk to you, after going there

3 -5 times, how could he know who if you are in an emergency?

I tend to like smaller churches better, that way I don't get lost in the flow.

Use these steps as a guide to finding a church home. If all of these work for you and you love the church, your next step is to get baptized!!!!

Why Baptism?

I'll start off with this: most of us have been Christened or baptized when we were babies or little. We had no idea of what was going on and many religions do this out of fear. From what I was taught, babies were made out of sin and the only way God would allow them into the kingdom of Heaven if they died was if they had been baptized or Christened.

This is petrifying!! Who wouldn't get their baby baptized? I was so convinced, that I even had my babies christened. I didn't want my babies to go to Hell. There are baby dedications, this is different from the baptisms and christenings. It is okay to dedicate the baby to The Lord, but water is not necessary.

A dedication is lifting the baby up to The Lord to protect them, guide their steps and that help them bring the child up in a Godly life.

There are two different types of Baptism.

1. The water baptism

This is usually done after you have said the prayer of salvation. Once you find the church you want to attend, you will need to ask about receiving this. The reasons are simple. First, it is a Biblical public statement that you have accepted The Lord as your Savior and that you have been cleansed from your sins and you are now a new creation. This will usually take place somewhere in the church and everyone watches and cheers.

Don't be scared! The pastor will not drown you. You are putting great joy in the Lords heart, acknowledging Him before all men! This really puts Satan in his place. It means more in the spirit than we will ever know. But, water is very important in the Bible. God made it and uses it! (Examples: parting the Red Sea, The Flood, the pigs cast into the sea with demons.) This is your 2nd biggest day!!! Make sure you write this day down. You will look back and smile every-time. Just remember, even Jesus was baptized.

Scripture references:

Matthew 3:13-17

The Baptism of Jesus

13 Then Jesus came from Galilee to the Jordan to be baptized by John. 14 But John tried to deter him, saying, "I need to be baptized by you, and do you come to me?"

15 Jesus replied, "Let it be so now; it is proper for us to do this to fulfill all righteousness." Then John consented.

16 As soon as Jesus was baptized, he went up out of the water. At that moment heaven was opened, and he saw the Spirit of God descending like a dove and alighting on him. 17 And a voice from heaven said, "This is my Son, whom I love; with him I am well pleased."

Acts 10:48

48 So he ordered that they be baptized in the name of Jesus Christ. Then they asked Peter to stay with them for a few days.

2. Baptism of the Holy Spirit

This is a baptism a lot of churches don't believe in. This is one of your biggest weapons, that's why Satan doesn't want anyone to use it!

We have a secret prayer language that God gives us. This prayer language is jumbled up and even in all different languages. But, when it is prayed, God knows the secret code! Sometimes in situations we just don't even know what to pray, but the Holy Spirit, who takes up residence in us, does! Satan cannot understand it! He understands our regular words and can try to use things against us or do things when he know what we are up to.

Not only does this prayer language go right to God's ears, but studies have been done and shown that there is another whole part of our brain being used when we do this. It has also been shown, that people who pray in this language heal quicker than people who don't. Now you see why Satan doesn't want us to use it or know about it.

We are all supposed to have it. I don't know about you, but anything I am supposed to have, I WANT! Pray this simple prayer out loud. Once you start praying something strange sounding may come out of your mouth. I have heard Chinese, Russian and all kinds of languages. It is good to pray like this everyday. That way the Holy Spirit can take it right to God.

The Holy Spirit Baptism Prayer:

If you do not know Jesus as your Savior and Lord, simply pray the following prayer in faith, and Jesus will be your Lord!

"Heavenly Father, I come to You in the Name of Jesus. Your Word says, 'Whosoever shall call on the name of the Lord shall be saved' (Acts2:21). I am calling on You. I pray and ask Jesus to come into my heart and be Lord over my life according to Romans 10:9-10: 'If thou shalt confess with thy mouth the Lord Jesus, and shalt believe in thine heart that God has raised him from the dead, thou shalt be saved. For with the heart man believeth unto righteousness; and with the mouth confession is made unto salvation.' I do that now. I confess that Jesus is Lord, and I believe in my heart that God raised Him from the dead.

"I am now reborn! I am a Christian—a child of Almighty God! I am saved! You also said in Your Word, 'If ye then being evil, know how to give good gifts unto your children: HOW MUCH MORE shall your heavenly Father give the Holy Spirit to them that ask him?' (Luke 11:13). I'm also asking You to fill me with the Holy Spirit. Holy Spirit, rise up within me as I praise God. I fully expect to speak with other tongues as You give me the utterance (Acts 2:4). In Jesus' Name. Amen!"

Begin to praise God for filling you with the Holy Spirit. Speak those words and syllables you receive—not in your own language, but the language given to you by the Holy Spirit. You have to use your own voice. God will not force you to speak. Don't be concerned with how it sounds. It is a heavenly language!

Continue with the blessing God has given you and pray in tongues each day. You are a born-again, Spirit-filled believer. You'll never be the same!
I borrowed this prayer from Kenneth Copeland Ministries. I am sure he won't mind that I borrowed it. He has great teachings on this subject. (You can find this on Kcm.org.)

Scripture reference:

Jude 1:20
20 But you, dear friends, by building yourselves up in your most holy faith and praying in the Holy Spirit,

Baptized on water date_____
Baptized in the Holy Spirit date_____

Finish equipping

A very important scripture you need to know and understand:

Ephesians 6:12
12 For our struggle is not against flesh and blood, but against the rulers, against the authorities, against the powers of this dark world and against the spiritual forces of evil in the heavenly realms.

Every bad thing that has happened to you in your life is explained in that scripture. It wasn't your dad that did that to you. It wasn't your friend that did that to you, it wasn't the husband. It was Satan who has come after you to steal, kill and destroy!

John 10:10
10 The thief comes only to steal and kill and destroy; I have come that they may have life, and have it to the full.

1 Peter 5:8
8 Be alert and of sober mind. Your enemy the devil prowls around like a roaring lion looking for someone to devour.

Three things that you need to do to prevent this:

1. Forgive every person that has ever been mean to you, hurt you, stolen from you or tried to destroy you.

It was not man that did these things to you. It was Satan using them against you! He knew that one day you might seek God's face. There is a battle that goes on around us daily. You have to forgive these people.

It is your own way that God will forgive you. You need to pray blessings on them. They don't have a clue they are being used. Neither did you while you were living the old life. How do you forgive them? It's not easy. Your flesh and Satan would like to see you stay stirred up so you won't have peace or freedom. I have sent cards to people that didn't even know I was mad. I have taken flowers to people. But, it's not about the objects - it's all about having a heart like His. If you don't forgive these people, God can't forgive you.

This is a scripture that everyone in the universe needs to know and do immediately! Highlight this one in your Bible:

Mark 11:25
25 And when you stand praying, if you hold anything against anyone, forgive them, so that your Father in heaven may forgive you your sins."

Write down everyone that has made you angry that you can remember. Now, look at each one and you see how the emotions get you all worked up. Look at each situation and recognize where Satan crept in and got in the middle. Don't be confused with the saying on the street, "Well, if it's God's will we will talk again". God wants us to talk and have friends and family. God didn't kill anyone, steal from anyone or lie to anyone.

Here is how I test the spirits. It's simple... If it's good it's from God and if it's not good it comes from the pit. By learning this and using this knowledge, you will be set free from so much old junk in the trunk! When you see this person, don't look at them like you did in the past. Recognize who is really responsible for the situation and clean it up. When you go back and work it out, you are punching Satan in the face.

2. The second weapon needed to fight Satan from trying to steal from you, kill or destroy is putting on the full Armor of God.

You need to cover yourself with this everyday. I speak it out loud.

Ephesians 6:11-18
11 Put on the full armor of God, so that you can take your stand against the devil's schemes. 12 For our struggle is not against flesh and blood, but against the rulers, against the authorities, against the powers of this dark world and against the spiritual forces of evil in the heavenly realms. 13 Therefore put on the full armor of God, so that when the day of evil comes, you may be able to stand your ground, and after you have done everything, to stand. 14 Stand firm then, with the belt of truth buckled around your waist, with the breastplate of righteousness in place, 15 and with your feet fitted with the readiness that comes from the gospel of peace. 16 In addition to all this, take up the shield of faith, with which you can extinguish all the flaming arrows of the evil one. 17 Take the helmet of salvation and the sword of the Spirit, which is the word of God. 18 And pray in the Spirit on all

occasions with all kinds of prayers and requests. With this in mind, be alert and always keep on praying for all the Lord's people.

The belt of truth is being equipped to recognize Satan's lies. Jesus came back to give us the truth and set us free from the power of Satan. The breastplate of righteousness is to activity tell the truth and good works. We are not righteousness without Jesus. The shield of faith combats all doubt, worry and fear. The sword of the spirit is using the word of God. When you use the sword, the enemy backs off. It has to be the exact word, nothing missing or added. Remember that Satan also knows the Word and likes to challenge us to see if we do. If we can't use the sword, we have nothing to fight back with. This is why you need to study the Bible. It is important to know who you are and what you have as the daughter or son of the King!

3. When you wake up in the morning, thank God for all that He has done and all that He has planned for your day.

Give Him your firsts. He loves it when you spend time with Him before anyone. Even if you can only do 10 minutes. do it! He will surprise you with wonderful things to get through your day. After I have spent my time with The Lord, I like to do what I say cleaning. I speak out of my mouth, that I cover my family, our health, prosperity, hope and future along with our jobs, finances, home, vehicles, safety and protection with the blood of Jesus.

I add things in daily to fit what is going on in my life. I don't do this prayer out of fear - I do it to remind Satan that Jesus covered all these things with His blood and therefore, Satan has to PASS OVER! He can't touch what Jesus covered in His blood.

Scripture reference:

Exodus12:13
13The blood shall be a sign for you on the houses where you live; and when I see the blood I will pass over you, and no plague will befall you to destroy you when I strike the land of Egypt.

What is your purpose?

We all have one. How can you know without asking? You can talk to your Heavenly Father like He is right next to you, because He is. Ask Him. He will reveal it.

Praying is the most important ministry. Even if you don't know how to pray, ask the Holy Spirit to help you. Pray over the government , the children, the teachers, your coworkers, your neighbors, your pastor. Pray for yourself. It's not bad to ask God for anything. He tells us to ask and you shall receive. Wherever you go, you are there on purpose. If you are in a doctors office, you may be the only person that prayed for a person dying and your prayer was answered and he was healed. You just don't know what your prayers are doing. Sometimes God will show us. You are a missionary where every you walk.

To have a deeper relationship with The Lord, you will need to give Him more of you and your time. He will reveal everything you need to know to live your life to the fullest and walk in the destiny calling He has for you.

If you could do anything for The Lord, what would you like to do? Write it down and visualize it. He will guide your steps. Keep a journal about how He uses you in ways that you never thought you could be used. It could turn into a book later.

What is the scariest thing that The Lord would have you do? Chances are this is where your calling is. Satan would like to make you think whatever this is, you can't do it.

I will be praying for every person that reads this book to be filled with the joy of The Lord and step into a deep, personal relationship with the One who loved you so much, He died on the cross for you. My prayer is that He will use you and He will be glorified! JESUS IS LORD! AMEN

Scripture references:

Philippians 4:6-7
6 Do not be anxious about anything, but in every situation, by prayer and petition, with thanksgiving, present your requests to God. 7 And the peace of God, which transcends all understanding, will guard your hearts and your minds in Christ Jesus.

Isaiah 61:1
1 The Spirit of the Sovereign Lord is on me, because the Lord has anointed me
to proclaim good news to the poor. He has sent me to bind up the brokenhearted,
to proclaim freedom for the captives and release from darkness for the prisoners,

Jeremiah 29:11
11 For I know the plans I have for you," declares the Lord, "plans to prosper you and not to harm you, plans to give you hope and a future.

8
ONE FINAL QUESTION

I went on a woman's retreat. In the morning I decided to take a walk on the trail before breakfast. I was praising God as I walked and the rays of light were coming thru the trees.

I told God, "I give you my entire heart."

As soon as I said that, I looked down and found a little red heart bead. I started to cry. I kept waking and came upon an outdoor altar. God spoke to me and said open your Bible and preach. I thought, *no one is here. But, I will do as He said.*

I opened my Bible and started to preach what I opened to. All of the sudden two squirrels came up and sat on the pews. I giggled and kept going. The next thing I noticed is two white ducks came up and stood by the pews. I laughed! I got done and looked at my watch. I needed to hurry back for the coffee, breakfast was about to end. I started to head out and when I was about to turn to go back, God spoke to me again: "Do you want the coffee or what I have waiting for you?"

I passed on the coffee and walked the other way. At the end of the path was a cross and water all around it except where I was standing. I fell to my knees and sobbed!

How many times do we follow our flesh and miss all that He has waiting for us?

What does He have waiting for YOU?

JOURNAL

Now is the time to take what you have read and turn this into your personal journey.

Take the next 60 days and read over the Scriptures and prayers in this book. Write down your thoughts. Be still and wait for God to speak to you.

Also use these journal pages to record how He uses you, how He blesses you, and how He challenges you to strive higher.

Find a quiet place and find at least 15 minutes each day to spend time with Him.

Keep this journal to look back in the years to come and see how far He has taken you.

Date: _____

_____
_____
_____
_____
_____
_____
_____
_____
_____
_____
_____
_____
_____
_____

Date: _____

_____
_____
_____
_____
_____
_____
_____
_____
_____
_____
_____
_____
_____
_____

Date: _____

_____
_____
_____
_____
_____
_____
_____
_____
_____
_____
_____
_____
_____

Date: _____

_____
_____
_____
_____
_____
_____
_____
_____
_____
_____
_____
_____
_____

Date: _____

_____
_____
_____
_____
_____
_____
_____
_____
_____
_____
_____
_____
_____
_____
_____

Date: _____

_____
_____
_____
_____
_____
_____
_____
_____
_____
_____
_____
_____
_____
_____
_____

Date: _____

_____
_____
_____
_____
_____
_____
_____
_____
_____
_____
_____
_____
_____
_____

Date: _____

_____
_____
_____
_____
_____
_____
_____
_____
_____
_____
_____
_____
_____
_____

Jill Wischhusen

Date: _____

_____

Date: _____

_____

80

Date: _____

_____
_____
_____
_____
_____
_____
_____
_____
_____
_____
_____
_____
_____
_____
_____

Date: _____

_____
_____
_____
_____
_____
_____
_____
_____
_____
_____
_____
_____
_____
_____

Date: _____

_____
_____
_____
_____
_____
_____
_____
_____
_____
_____
_____
_____

Date: _____

_____
_____
_____
_____
_____
_____
_____
_____
_____
_____
_____
_____
_____

Date: _____

_____
_____
_____
_____
_____
_____
_____
_____
_____
_____
_____
_____
_____
_____
_____

Date: _____

_____
_____
_____
_____
_____
_____
_____
_____
_____
_____
_____
_____
_____
_____
_____

Date: _____

_____
_____
_____
_____
_____
_____
_____
_____
_____
_____
_____
_____
_____
_____

Date: _____

_____
_____
_____
_____
_____
_____
_____
_____
_____
_____
_____
_____
_____
_____

Date: _____

_____
_____
_____
_____
_____
_____
_____
_____
_____
_____
_____
_____
_____
_____

Date: _____

_____
_____
_____
_____
_____
_____
_____
_____
_____
_____
_____
_____
_____
_____

Date: _____

_____
_____
_____
_____
_____
_____
_____
_____
_____
_____
_____
_____
_____
_____

Date: _____

_____
_____
_____
_____
_____
_____
_____
_____
_____
_____
_____
_____
_____
_____

Date: _____

_____
_____
_____
_____
_____
_____
_____
_____
_____
_____
_____
_____
_____
_____

Date: _____

_____
_____
_____
_____
_____
_____
_____
_____
_____
_____
_____
_____
_____
_____
_____
_____

Date: _____

_____
_____
_____
_____
_____
_____
_____
_____
_____
_____
_____
_____
_____
_____

Date: _____

_____
_____
_____
_____
_____
_____
_____
_____
_____
_____
_____
_____
_____
_____

Date: _____

_____
_____
_____
_____
_____
_____
_____
_____
_____
_____
_____
_____
_____
_____

Date: _____

_____
_____
_____
_____
_____
_____
_____
_____
_____
_____
_____
_____
_____
_____

Date: _____

_____

_____

_____

_____

_____

_____

_____

_____

_____

_____

_____

_____

_____

Date: _____

_____

_____

_____

_____

_____

_____

_____

_____

_____

_____

_____

_____

_____

Date: _____

_____
_____
_____
_____
_____
_____
_____
_____
_____
_____
_____
_____
_____

Date: _____

_____
_____
_____
_____
_____
_____
_____
_____
_____
_____
_____
_____
_____

Date: _____

_____
_____
_____
_____
_____
_____
_____
_____
_____
_____
_____
_____
_____
_____

Date: _____

_____
_____
_____
_____
_____
_____
_____
_____
_____
_____
_____
_____
_____
_____

Date: _____

_____
_____
_____
_____
_____
_____
_____
_____
_____
_____
_____
_____
_____
_____

Date: _____

_____
_____
_____
_____
_____
_____
_____
_____
_____
_____
_____
_____
_____
_____

Date: _____

_____
_____
_____
_____
_____
_____
_____
_____
_____
_____
_____
_____
_____

Date: _____

_____
_____
_____
_____
_____
_____
_____
_____
_____
_____
_____
_____
_____
_____

Date: _____

_____
_____
_____
_____
_____
_____
_____
_____
_____
_____
_____
_____
_____

Date: _____

_____
_____
_____
_____
_____
_____
_____
_____
_____
_____
_____
_____
_____

Date: _____

_____
_____
_____
_____
_____
_____
_____
_____
_____
_____
_____
_____
_____
_____

Date: _____

_____
_____
_____
_____
_____
_____
_____
_____
_____
_____
_____
_____
_____
_____
_____

Date: _____

_____
_____
_____
_____
_____
_____
_____
_____
_____
_____
_____
_____
_____
_____

Date: _____

_____
_____
_____
_____
_____
_____
_____
_____
_____
_____
_____
_____
_____
_____

Date: _____

_____
_____
_____
_____
_____
_____
_____
_____
_____
_____
_____
_____
_____
_____

Date: _____

_____
_____
_____
_____
_____
_____
_____
_____
_____
_____
_____
_____
_____
_____

Date: _____

_____
_____
_____
_____
_____
_____
_____
_____
_____
_____
_____
_____
_____
_____
_____

Date: _____

_____
_____
_____
_____
_____
_____
_____
_____
_____
_____
_____
_____
_____
_____

Date: _____

_____
_____
_____
_____
_____
_____
_____
_____
_____
_____
_____
_____
_____
_____

Date: _____

_____
_____
_____
_____
_____
_____
_____
_____
_____
_____
_____
_____
_____
_____

Date: _____

_____
_____
_____
_____
_____
_____
_____
_____
_____
_____
_____
_____
_____
_____

Date: _____

_____
_____
_____
_____
_____
_____
_____
_____
_____
_____
_____
_____
_____
_____

Date: _____

_____
_____
_____
_____
_____
_____
_____
_____
_____
_____
_____
_____
_____

Date: _____

_____
_____
_____
_____
_____
_____
_____
_____
_____
_____
_____
_____
_____

egmentation: body

Date: _____

_____
_____
_____
_____
_____
_____
_____
_____
_____
_____
_____
_____
_____
_____

Date: _____

_____
_____
_____
_____
_____
_____
_____
_____
_____
_____
_____
_____
_____
_____

Date: _____

_____
_____
_____
_____
_____
_____
_____
_____
_____
_____
_____
_____
_____
_____

Date: _____

_____
_____
_____
_____
_____
_____
_____
_____
_____
_____
_____
_____
_____
_____

Date: _____

_____

_____

_____

_____

_____

_____

_____

_____

_____

_____

_____

_____

_____

_____

Date: _____

_____

_____

_____

_____

_____

_____

_____

_____

_____

_____

_____

_____

_____

_____

FOR MORE INFORMATION

To learn more about Jill, her journey, and her ministry (to the Ukraine and more!), visit her site:

www.PrayerWarriorJill.weebly.com

Do you have a story to share?

At Rockhold Publishing, we love sharing stories that inspire, encourage, and enlighten.

We work with individuals and groups.

If you would like information about sharing your story, please visit

www.RockholdPublishing.com

If you have a church or ministry, please go to

www.RockholdPublishing.com/churches.html

Made in the USA
Middletown, DE
03 March 2021

34596683R00066